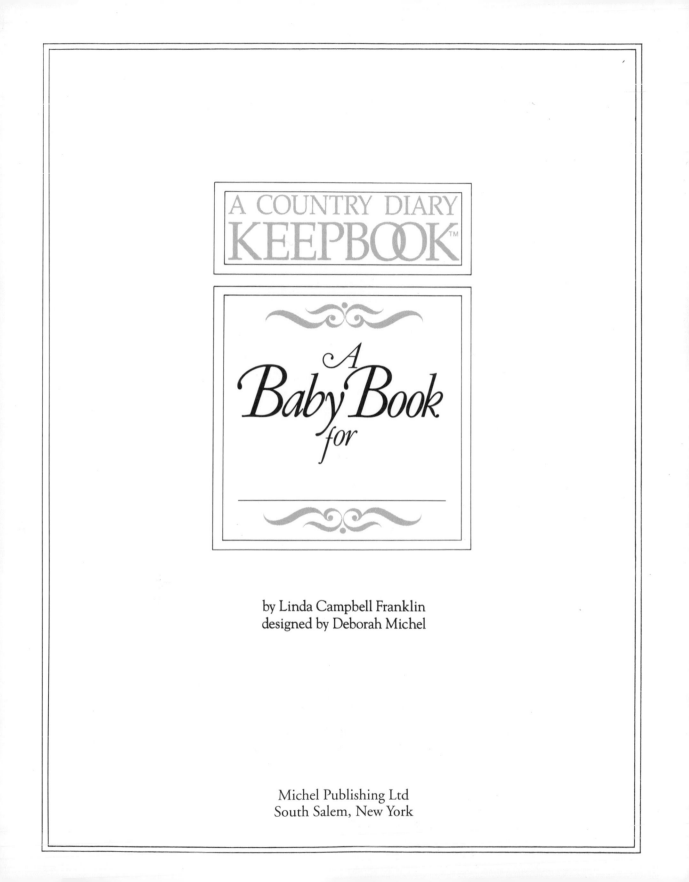

A COUNTRY DIARY
KEEPBOOK™

A
Baby Book
for

by Linda Campbell Franklin
designed by Deborah Michel

Michel Publishing Ltd
South Salem, New York

Published in the United States by
Michel Publishing, LTD.
3 Forest Street, New Canaan, CT 06840

Manufactured in China by
South China Printing Company.
(1988) Limited

BB100 / 170197 / 5

Special thanks to William Marmon,
of Ivy, Virginia, for the inspiration of
the baby book kept for him by his
mother.

Cover illustration by Judith Sutton

ISBN 0-934504-90-3

Dear Mothers and Fathers,

You have started a biography-keepbook that will become a family treasure. My parents kept such a book, and presented it to me on my sixteenth birthday. It was filled with notes and drawings and mementos that revealed to me my babyhood. I have found it intriguing to go back to and read, again and again. This baby book will hold the same kind of surprises and revelations for your child, thirteen, or sixteen, or twenty-one years from now!

The advice I got from expectant parents, and what I learned from looking at my book and the wonderfully-stuffed baby book lent me by a friend, is that we must provide you with plenty of space for writing, as well as room for photographs and souvenirs. We hope we've given you enough of both. And if your baby book becomes filled to overflowing with clippings and cards and notes left by the babysitter, don't worry, all baby books look the same way. Just tie it up with ribbon.

Best Wishes,

Linda Campbell Franklin

This book is dedicated to

_____

and to all
the babies
who will have their
biographies written

Contents

great-grandmother
birthplace _____
birth date _____

great-grandmother
birthplace _____
birth date _____

great-grandfather
birthplace _____
birth date _____

great-grandfather
birthplace _____
birth date _____

paternal
grandfather
birthplace _____
birth date _____

paternal
grandmother
birthplace _____
birth date _____

father
birthplace _____
birth date _____

baby
birthplace _____
birth date _____

The Family Tree

great-grandmother

birthplace _____

birth date _____

great-grandmother

birthplace _____

birth date _____

great-grandfather

birthplace _____

birth date _____

great-grandfather

birthplace _____

birth date _____

maternal
grandfather

birthplace _____

birth date _____

maternal
grandmother

birthplace _____

birth date _____

mother

birthplace _____

birth date _____

Dreams for Our Baby

Mother's

As the baby's mother, my hope is

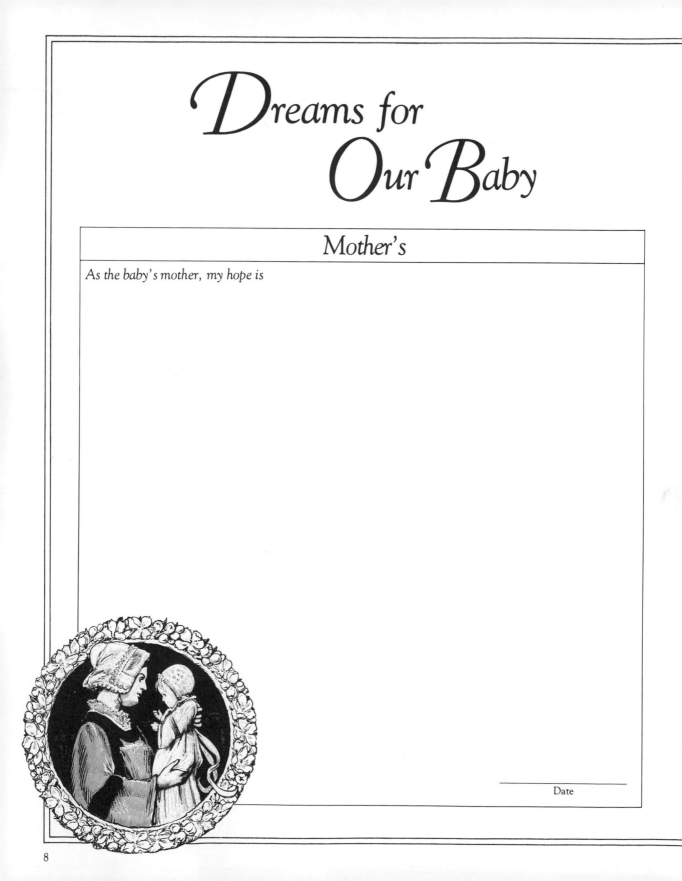

Date

Father's

As the baby's father, I have a dream that

_____ Date

Birth Announcement

Born on _____ the _____ day of _____, 19 _____

at _____ o'clock _____ a.m. _____ p.m.

Place _____

Doctor/Midwife _____

Nurse _____

Notes _____

_____

_____

_____

_____

_____

_____

Birth Announcement Card

Paste here.
Cellophane tape does not last.

Newspaper Announcement

Paste here.

Congratulations

Telegrams & Notes

Telegrams & Notes

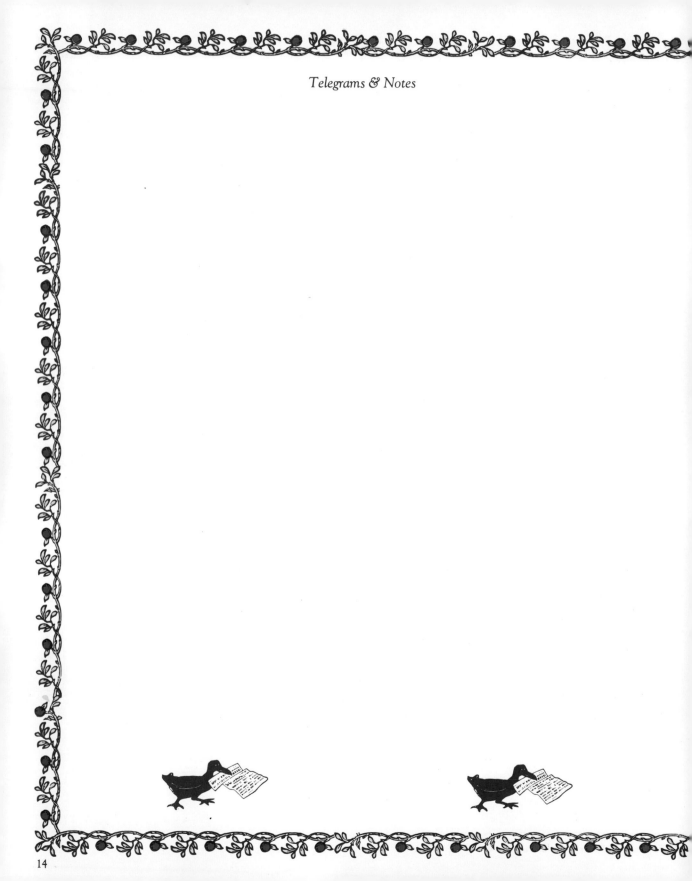

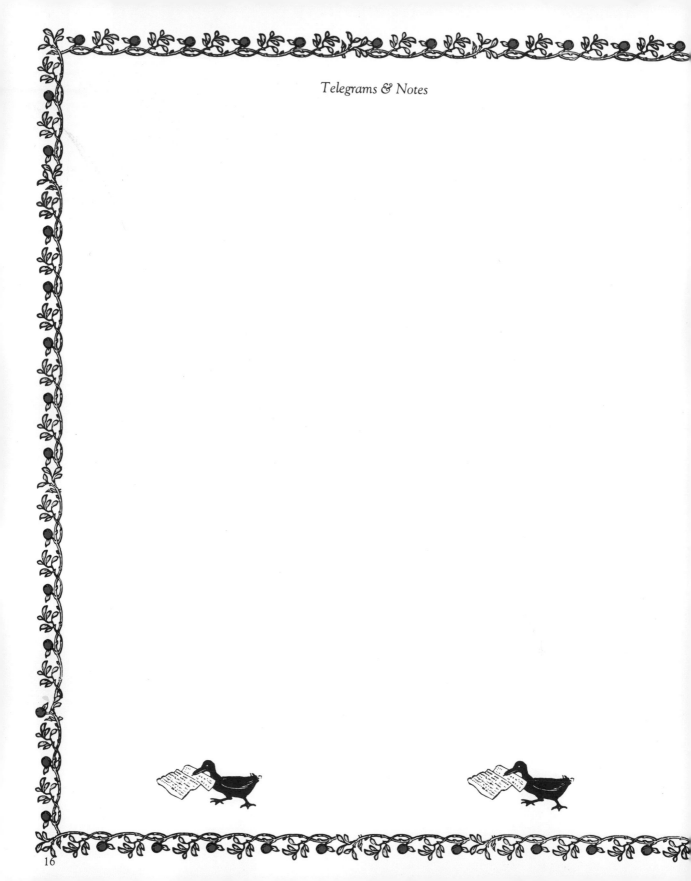

Telegrams & Notes

TO DARLING BABY

How Baby Looks

Color of eyes at birth _____ Color of eyes later _____

Color of hair _____ and eyebrows _____ and eyelashes _____

Shape of head _____ Circumference of head _____ inches

Weight _____ pounds _____ ounces   Height _____ inches

Resemblance to relatives _____

_____

_____

Birth Certificate

Paste one copy here.
Keep the other in a safe place.

Baby's First Pictures

Baby Goes Home

Baby went home on _____ at _____ o'clock _____ a.m. _____ p.m.

The trip was made by _____

The address of baby's first home is _____

_____

_____

Who was at home to welcome baby _____

_____

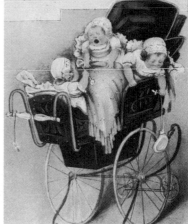

Just to keep your hand in,
A job you can't go wrong with
To occupy your overtime;
ENOUGH TO PUSH ALONG WITH.

Paste picture of mother and baby here.

Paste picture of your home here.

25

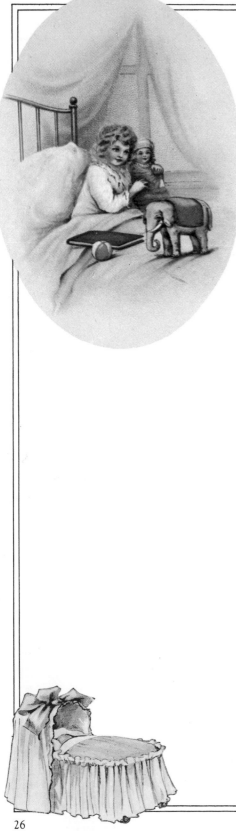

Paste picture of cradle or crib here.

Paste picture of room here

Baby's Realm

The nursery is in _____

We fixed it up in pretty colors, _____

here is a description of how it looks _____

_____

_____

_____

Here is a list of all baby's special nursery furniture and equipment _____

_____

_____

_____

_____

_____

Baby's Layette

Handmade Especially for _____

_____ by _____

_____ by _____

_____ by _____

_____ by _____

_____ by _____

_____ by _____

_____ by _____

_____ by _____

_____ by _____

_____ by _____

_____ by _____

_____ by _____

Drawstring sacques and shirts that snap;
Pretty blankets for a nap.
Fluffy ducks and gingham dogs
Play on baby's tiny togs.
Yellow and green, blue and pink,
Baby's layette is darling, don't you think?

The Rest of Baby's Layette

The Newspapers on the Day of Birth

Local Headlines

(Remember, if you want a record of what happened on the day the baby was born, use headlines, etc., from the next day's paper.)

The name of the newspaper

National Headlines

World Headlines

Weather

Sports News

A Champion Baby

_____ may never be a football quarterback,
Or a silver cup-winner at tennis or track,
Or break two hundred, in eighteen holes,
Or gain recognition for the way _____ bowls,
Or follow in the footsteps of a marathon runner.
But reading about 'em—what could be funner?

Fashions of the Day

Clip and paste in pictures of fashions being worn
    By women, men and children, at the time the baby's born.
Take them from magazines, or newspaper ads,
    Not only the classics, but also the fads!

Plays and Movies

Paste advertisements, schedules or reviews here.

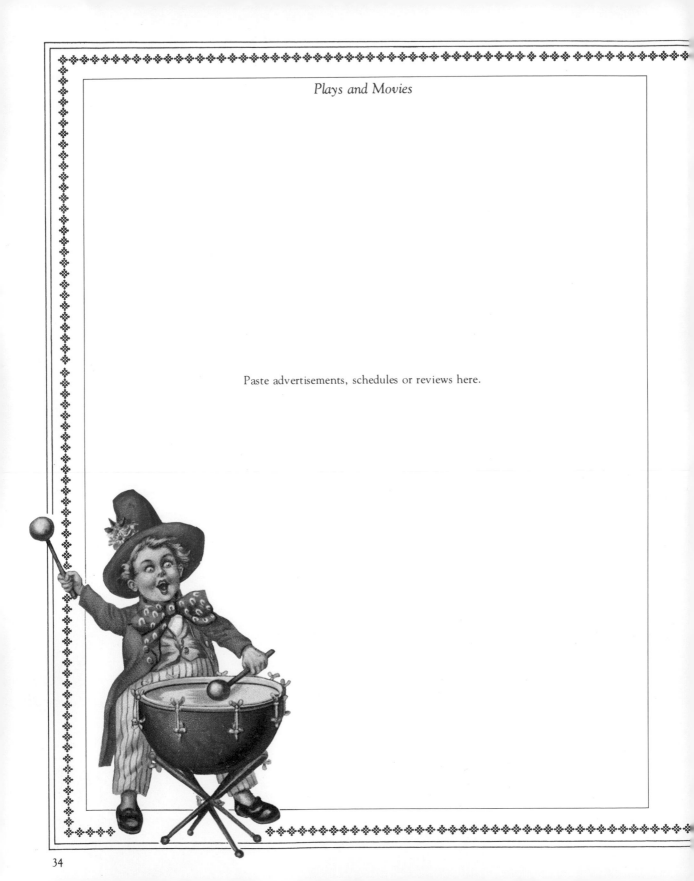

That's Entertainment!

Radio and Television Shows

Paste schedules or reviews here.

Best Sellers!

Books

The Top of the Charts!

Albums, Tapes & Singles

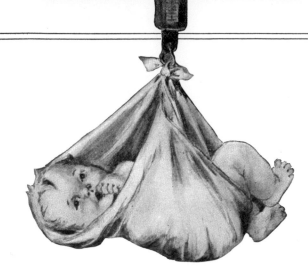

I'm aweigh just now-
See you later

THE FIRST YEAR

											WEEKS														
LBS.	1	2	3	4	6	8	10	12	14	16	18	20	22	24	26	28	30	32	34	36	38	40	42	44	46	48	50	52
24																												
23																												
22																												
21																												
20																												
19																												
18																												
17																												
16																												
15																												
14																												
13																												
12																												
11																												
10																												
9																												
8																												
7																												
6																												
5																												

*W*eight *C*harts

THE SECOND YEAR																										
WEEKS																										
LBS.	53	55	57	59	61	63	65	67	69	71	73	75	77	79	81	83	85	87	89	91	93	95	97	99	101	103	105
34																											
33																											
32																											
31																											
30																											
29																											
28																											
27																											
26																											
25																											
24																											
23																											
22																											
21																											
20																											
19																											
18																											
17																											
16																											
15																											

For the first year, the chart is divided so that after the first four weeks you record the weight of your baby once every two weeks (as in the second year chart). Put a dot on the correct intersection of weight and week and then connect the dots.

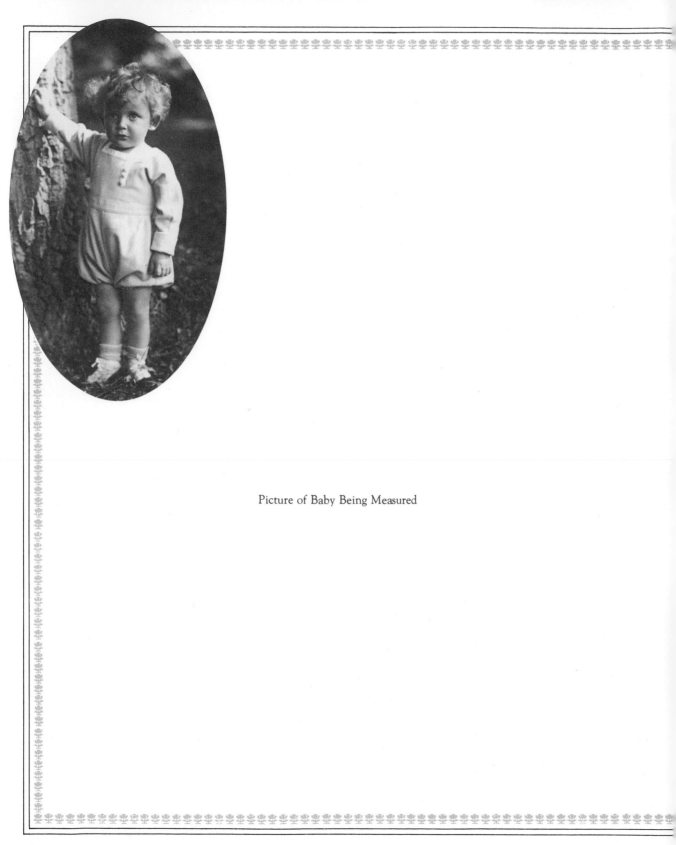

Picture of Baby Being Measured

Height Chart

At birth _____

One week _____

Two weeks _____

One month _____

Two months _____

Three months _____

Four months _____

Five months _____

Six months _____

Seven months _____

Eight months _____

Nine months _____

Ten months _____

Eleven months _____

One year _____

Fifteen months _____

Eighteen months _____

Twenty-one months _____

Two years _____

Visits to the Doctor

Doctor _____

Date _____ Comments _____

Doctor _____

Date _____ Comments _____

Doctor _____

Date _____ Comments _____

Doctor _____

Date _____ Comments _____

Doctor _____

Date _____ Comments _____

Doctor _____

Date _____ Comments _____

Doctor _____

Date _____ Comments _____

Doctor _____

Date _____ Comments _____

Doctor _____

Date _____ Comments _____

Doctor _____

Date _____ Comments _____

Doctor _____

Date _____ Comments _____

Doctor _____

Date _____ Comments _____

Doctor _____

Date _____ Comments _____

Doctor _____

Date _____ Comments _____

Immunizations

_____ Date _____ Booster _____

_____ Date _____ Booster _____

_____ Date _____ Booster _____

_____ Date _____ Booster _____

_____ Date _____ Booster _____

_____ Date _____ Booster _____

_____ Date _____ Booster _____

Feeding the *Baby*

Feeding Schedule
First month
Second month
Third month
Fourth month
Fifth month
Sixth month
Seventh month
Eighth month
Ninth month
Tenth month
Eleventh month
Twelfth month
Thirteenth to Eighteenth months
Nineteenth to Twenty-four months
Solid Foods

Formula

Pat-a-cake, pat-a-cake, baker's man!
Bake me a cake, fast as you can;
Pat it and prick it, and mark it with a "B,"
And put it in the oven for baby and me.

Paste picture of baby being fed here.

_____
Date

Baby's First Haircut

Paste picture of first haircut here.

Won't Mama be pleased.

_____
Date

46

Describe the Event

Paste envelope here for first lock of hair.

Baby Tooth Chart

_____
Central Incisor

_____
Lateral Incisor

_____
Cuspid

_____
First Molar

_____
Second Molar

_____
Second Molar

_____
First Molar

_____
Cuspid

_____
Lateral Incisor

_____
Central Incisor

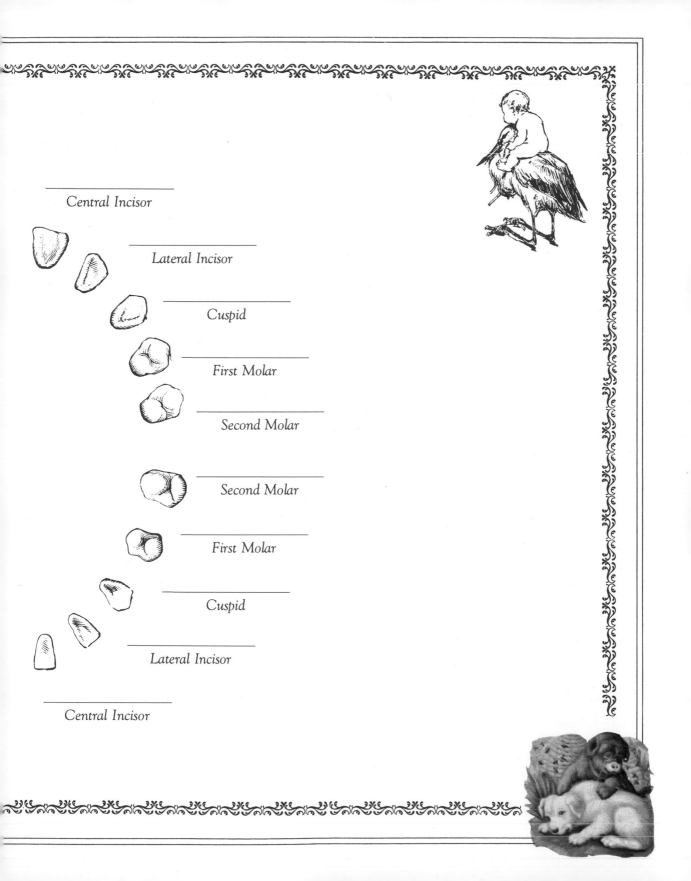

Central Incisor

Lateral Incisor

Cuspid

First Molar

Second Molar

Second Molar

First Molar

Cuspid

Lateral Incisor

Central Incisor

Firsts

Our baby, _____, will do many things,
  Over and over again.
Here is recorded what _____ did first,
  And also exactly when.

Holds cup and drinks _____

Eats solid food _____

Holds spoon _____

Throws something _____

Reaches for things _____

Sits up without help _____

Stands up _____

Walks _____

Speaks a word _____

The word is _____

Pulls off hat or socks _____

Bath _____

Sleeps through night _____

Smiles _____

Laughs _____

Kicks vigorously _____

Holds head up _____

Creeps _____

Crawls _____

Turns over _____

Finds feet and hands _____

Recognizes parents _____

Recognizes relatives _____

Babbles and coos _____

Holds bottle _____

Other firsts _____

_____

_____

_____

_____

_____

_____

_____

Gallery of First Time Photos

Baby's Toys

The First Toy

The Favorite Toy

What the baby calls it

Stuffed Animals

Dolls

Bouncing Toys

Pull-toys

Toys that Hang

This little piggy went to market;
This little piggy stayed home;
This little piggy had roast beef;
This little piggy had none;
And this little piggy cried "Wee, wee, wee!"
   All the way home.

How Baby Plays

Paste picture of baby playing here.

Beddy-bye & Lullabies

_____'s Favorite Lullaby

Who sings it?

Where do they sit?

Hush-a-bye, baby, on the tree top;
   When the wind blows, the cradle will rock;
When the bough bends, the cradle will fall;
   Down will come baby, cradle and all.

Sleeping Schedule

Hushy baby, my doll, I pray you don't cry,
    And I'll give you some bread and some milk, by-and-by.
Or perhaps you like custard, or maybe a tart—
Then to either you're welcome, with all of my heart.

Baby Showers

Paste pictures, souvenirs, favors or invitations here.

Who gave it? _____

Where? _____

When? _____

Gifts _____

_____

_____

_____

Who gave it? _____

Where? _____

When? _____

Gifts _____

_____

_____

_____

Who gave it? _____

Where? _____

When? _____

Gifts _____

_____

_____

_____

Portraits

Baby

Paste picture here.

Can you see the resemblances?

Parents

Paste picture here.

The Nine Months Before Birth

Parents' Diary: Notes & Feelings
First month
Second month
Third month
Fourth month
Fifth month
Sixth month
Seventh month
Eighth month
The last few weeks

Mother's Weight Chart

Pounds Gained	Months								
	1	2	3	4	5	6	7	8	9
29									
28									
27									
26									
25									
24									
23									
22									
21									
20									
19									
18									
17									
16									
15									
14									
13									
12									
11									
10									
9									
8									
7									
6									
5									
4									
3									
2									
1									
Start ⟶									

Enter your weight when you first knew in the "start" box. Weigh yourself the same day every month and enter in correct box.

What Mother Can Feel

I felt the first flutter of life on _____

_____

_____

I felt the first kicks on _____

_____

_____

The baby's father felt the kicks too, on _____

_____

_____

I felt the first hiccups on _____

_____

_____

I was able to listen to the heartbeats today _____

_____

_____

The baby's father heard them too, on _____

_____

_____

Record here a day of baby's movements

Mother and Baby
Grow & Grow

First Month

Second Month

At first the change is very slow,
When baby first begins to grow.
As mother gets a little rounder,
        here and there,
Father loves her even more,
        and shows her special care.
    The pictures, taken from one side, or the other,
        Show how baby keeps on getting bigger,
            inside mother!

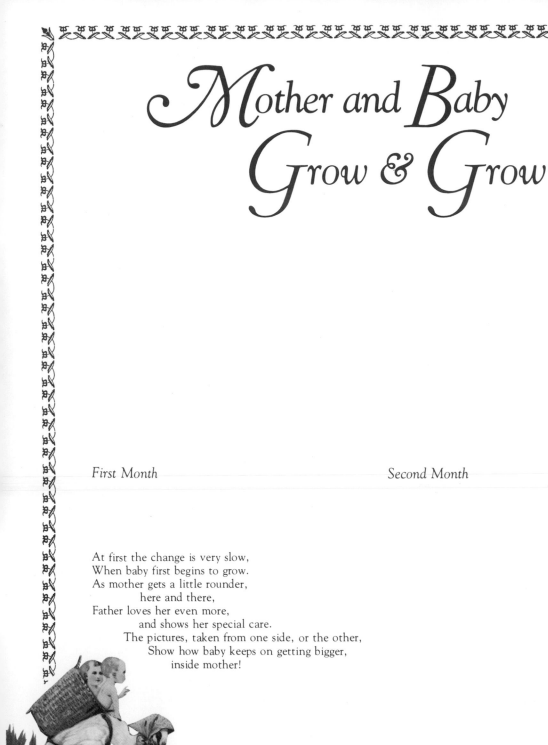

Third Month

Fourth Month

Fifth Month

Sixth Month

Seventh Month

Eighth Month

Ninth Month

Mother's Diary

Pre-natal Classes

Breathing Exercises

What I Must Do at Home

What My Husband is Supposed to Do

During pregnancy, my favorite foods were

Everyone is supposed to crave pickles and ice cream, and I craved

The music I listened to most was

Other entertainments were

Doctor Visits

Doctor's Name _____

Date _____

Comments _____

_____

Date _____

Comments _____

_____

Date _____

Comments _____

_____

Date _____

Comments _____

_____

Date _____

Comments _____

_____

Date _____

Comments _____

_____

Date _____

Comments _____

_____

Date _____

Comments _____

_____

Date _____

Comments _____

_____

Date _____

Comments _____

_____

Date _____

Comments _____

_____

Date _____

Comments _____

_____

Date _____   Date _____

Comments _____   Comments _____

_____   _____

Date _____   Date _____

Comments _____   Comments _____

_____   _____

Date _____   Date _____

Comments _____   Comments _____

_____   _____

Date _____   Date _____

Comments _____   Comments _____

_____   _____

Date _____   Date _____

Comments _____   Comments _____

_____   _____

Date _____   Date _____

Comments _____   Comments _____

_____   _____

Date _____   Date _____

Comments _____   Comments _____

Books We Read
on Baby Care

Title _____

Author _____

Quotes or comments _____

_____

Title _____

Author _____

Quotes or comments _____

_____

Title _____

Author _____

Quotes or comments _____

_____

Title _____

Author _____

Quotes and comments _____

_____

Title _____

Author _____

Quotes or comments _____

_____

Title _____

Author _____

Quotes or comments _____

_____

Title _____

Author _____

Quotes or comments _____

_____

Title _____

Author _____

Quotes or comments _____

_____

The Day Before the Birth

How We Spent the Day Before

What We Were Doing When THE TIME Came!

The time was _____ o'clock __ a.m. __ p.m.

What Was Packed in My Suitcase

Names for Baby

Mother's Ideas

Father's Ideas

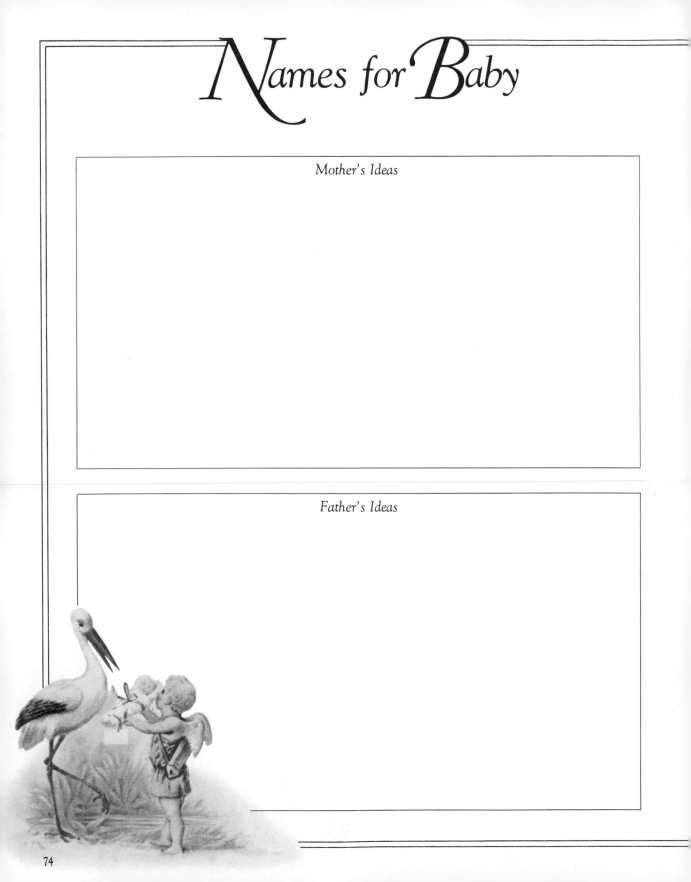

Ideas from the Rest of the Family

Everyone, but everyone, thinks they've got the perfect name.
To the baby, of course, it's all the same.
It's when the child is older, the matter's inflated,
So take care! You want your choice appreciated.

A Word in Baby's Ear

The uncles and the aunts,
  The sisters and the brothers,
The cousins in the short pants,
  And all and any others
Say something clever in rhyme,
  or something ad-lib
When they first see the infant
  in its crib.

Family Quotes on Our Baby

Pictures of the Whole Family

Paste picture here.

Paste cards here.

Baby's First Birthday

Who Came to the Party _____

_____

_____

_____

_____

What We Had to Eat _____

_____

_____

_____

Gifts _____

_____

_____

_____

Short Birthday Messages _____

_____

_____

_____

The Newspapers on the First Birthday

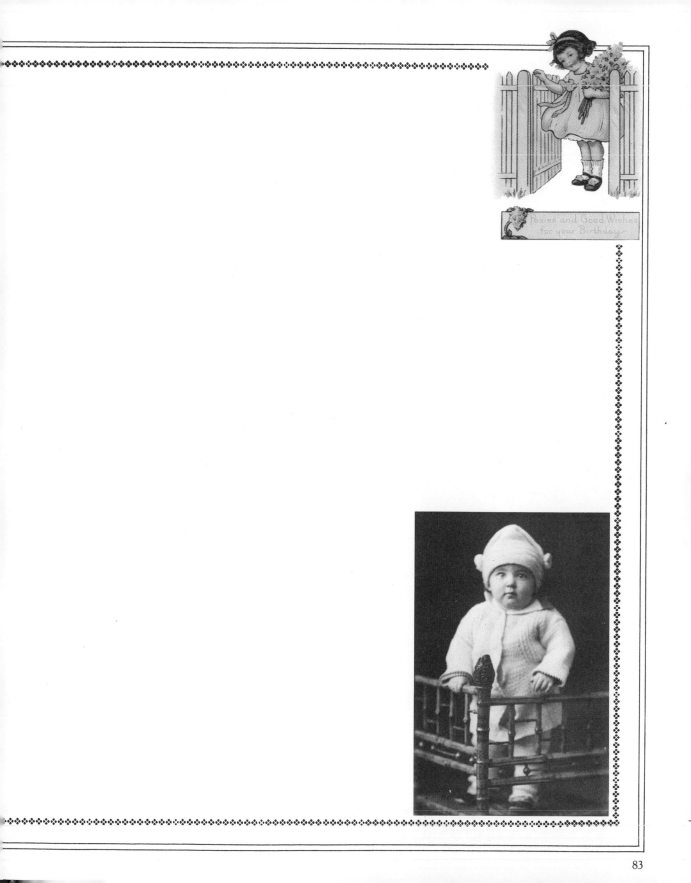

Posies and Good Wishes
for your Birthday

Developing Habits

Thumb-sucking _____

_____

Lip-sucking _____

_____

Sucking of toys, blankets, etc. _____

_____

Dirt-eating _____

_____

Head-banging _____

_____

Breath-holding _____

_____

Tantrums _____

_____

Food-throwing _____

_____

Toy-dropping _____

_____

Bouncing and jouncing _____

_____

Other _____

_____

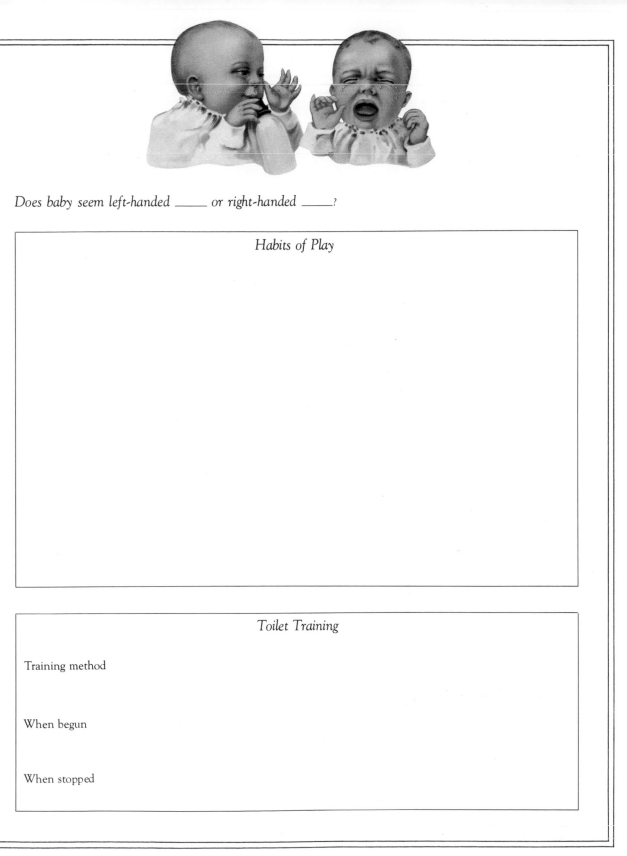

Does baby seem left-handed _____ *or right-handed* _____?

Habits of Play

Toilet Training

Training method

When begun

When stopped

Baby's first syllables

Baby's first words

Baby's first sentences

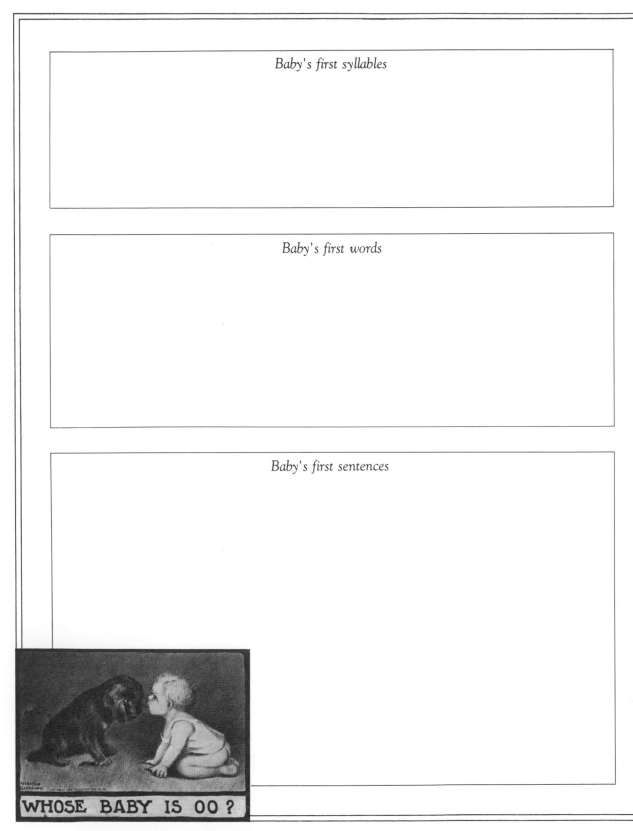

WHOSE BABY IS OO ?

Language Development

Vocabulary at a Year and a Half

Vocabulary at Two Years

Baby's First Trips

Paste picture here.

We went _____

on _____ . We _____

_____

_____

We went _____

on _____ . We _____

_____

_____

We went _____

on _____ . We _____

_____

_____

We went _____

on _____ . We _____

_____

_____

We went _____

on _____ . We _____

_____

Memorable Occasions

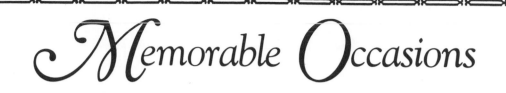

Baby's Second Birthday

Paste picture here.

Paste picture here.

Who Was at the Celebration

What We Had to Eat

Gifts

Bye-Bye

Paste picture of baby waving goodbye here.

_____
Date